Beyond the Names Chart

Using Children's Names for Word Study

by Debbie Diller

Teaching Resource Center

My mission is to live with courage and conviction
to inspire and empower teachers to see each child's
unique gifts, to value children's differences, and to use
these to teach ALL children to read, write, and think.

Teaching Resource Center
P.O. Box 82777
San Diego, CA 92138

Edited by
Design and production by Janis Poe
Illustrations by Linda Starr

Printed in the United States of America
ISBN: 1-56785-059-6

Contents

Introduction

Beyond the Names Chart: Using Children's Names for Word Study is based on my work as a literacy coach in many preschool through second grade classrooms over the years. I often see teachers using children's names for the first few weeks of school. This rich word study can continue throughout the year and doesn't have to end after we've studied each child's name for a day!

This book is written to help teachers use names powerfully to teach children how words work. It is centered around word study (phonics and spelling instruction) connected to the most important piece of text for a child—his or her name.

You can use names to help beginning writers. For instance, young children can write their names as part of the news each day, as shown here.

You can also help students use their names and the names of classmates to transfer principles of how words work. More advanced readers might make a name web, like the one pictured below. Note the useful chunks in *Alexander (al, ex, and, er)* that can be applied to new words the child is trying to read and write. Known words generated by the child are links to help him remember these parts of his name to solve new words in reading and writing. This names chart might be kept in the child's reading folder and used as the teacher prompts the child to remember.

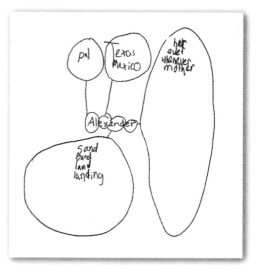

The child's name is the first word he/she learns to read and write. It can be used to teach letter formation and letter identification, too. Every child should learn to read and write her name and the names of classmates. Most letters can be learned in this way. Teachers can use children's names all year long, extending names work to last names and even middle names as children move through the primary grades.

Children love seeing and hearing their names. In this book, you will find a teaching framework for weaving names work across the day and throughout the year. When children's learning is connected and continuous, they find it easier to remember! Use the ideas in this book to help your students learn how their names work and how these principles can apply to other words they are learning.

Using a Names Chart

I put a names chart in my classroom at the beginning of school. I teach with names during the first month of school. Isn't that enough?

A names chart is a great place to begin! And beyond the names chart, lots of powerful teaching can take place. Names can help students with phonics and spelling. Names can also increase awareness of culture and history. Learning each other's names helps to build a community of learners.

Use *Names Around the Room* on page 6 to help you see the many possibilities for using children's names around the classroom. Add photos to your names charts using a regular or digital camera, or use the small photos that come with students' school pictures.

There are many ways to make names charts. The chart shown is made with a piece of stiff discount fabric (25" x 36"). Black felt cut into 2¼" x 6½" strips were glued to the fabric. Each name was typed with Comic Sans, font size 72 bold, and printed onto white cardstock and laminated. Then a small piece of Velcro was attached to the back of each name card so it can be removed by the teacher or children. The photo was added in the same way. Precut fun foam figures were glued onto the fabric to make a colorful border. This names chart is interactive and can be used year after year.

Another simple way to create a names chart is to print or type each child's name onto a card and place it in a pocket chart. Use print large enough for all children to see easily. Names cards and photos can also be glued to poster board to create a names chart. Place the large names chart in your large group teaching area near your big book easel and the place where you write with children so you can use it for teaching. Also make smaller 8½" x 11" names charts for use in small groups.

2nd grade note:
Use first and last names on your names charts.

Working with Children's Names

When working with a names chart, here are some questions you might ask students to invite investigation about their names. These might be asked again as you add middle or last names to the chart throughout the year. Choose appropriate questions to match the development of students in your classroom.

- What do you notice about this name?

- How many letters does it have?

- How many tall letters?

- How many short letters?

- How many letters with sticks?

- How many letters with circles?

- How many letters with dots?

- How many ___'s? (name a letter)

- How many capital letters does it have?

- How many parts does this name have? Clap it. Count the parts.

- Does it look like anyone else's name?

- How does it look like that name?

- Does it sound like anyone else's name?

- How does it sound like that name?

- Do you see any chunks you know?

- Does anyone else have those same chunks in their name?

Special Walls with Names

The classroom library is a great place for a special kind of names chart. Take a photo of each child and enlarge it. (If you use a digital camera, you can use the picture toolbar in Microsoft Word to crop the photo.) Cut around the shape of the child's head to create a cutout. Fasten it to the wall in your classroom library and attach a speech bubble that includes the child's name and what he or she says about books and reading. Children will delight in using this unique names chart.

Brittany says, "I like to read books about Barbie."

Many teachers also place children's names on the word wall beginning the first weeks of school. Once those names are on the wall, children should be held accountable for spelling them correctly. Teach them how to access the names (and other words) from the word wall throughout the year. When you can make the word wall interactive, children will use it even more. Many teachers are using their magnetic chalkboards for their word walls and then attaching a small piece of magnetic tape to the back of each name/word. This way children can take words off the wall to copy them, sort them, etc.

Rudy says, "My favorite book is 'I'm the King of the Mountains' by Joy Cowley."

2nd grade note:

Use first and last names on your word wall. Place first names and last names separately on the word wall. You might use different colors for each.

Names Around the Room

The classroom belongs to your students. Celebrate them by using their names everywhere! Be sure their names are big and bold. Use black print in an easy-to-read font, such as Comic Sans. Include names on cards, big charts, small charts, and sentence strips, as shown below. Use the checklist on page 7 to see if you have used kids' names to their maximum potential.

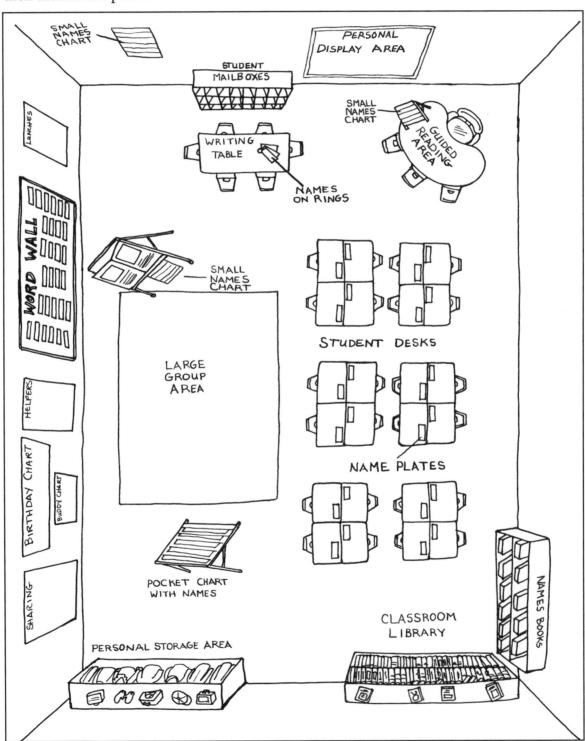

Names Checklist

Do you have large, easy-to-read names...?

WHERE?	WHY?	YES or NO
On desks or tables for each child	To show letter formation; to aid in name recognition	
On the word wall	To use as spelling resources	
On a lunch chart	To promote student independence with classroom routines; to recognize names	
On a helpers chart	To promote student independence with classroom routines; to recognize names	
On a birthday chart	To provide a reference for spelling children's names and months of the year	
On a sharing chart	To teach sharing and responsibility	
On a buddy chart	To teach organization and classroom routines	
On hangers or cubbies for each child	To teach organization and responsibility	
On sentence strips in the pocket chart	To teach phonics and spelling; to build community	
On a chart in the classroom library	For print awareness; to share favorite books and build community	
On a small chart in the guided reading area	To provide a reference for phonics and spelling	
Labeling a personal display area	To showcase each child's best work; to build community	

Teaching with Names in Read Aloud

Use picture books that highlight names throughout the year during read aloud. You might place a plastic tub in your classroom library and label it *Names Books*, as shown. As you read aloud these books, add them to the container for students to read on their own. You might put a colored dot on the tub and on each book in the tub to help children put the books back in the correct container.

Use these read aloud books to talk and write about names. (This doesn't all have to happen the first two weeks of school. Names are interesting all year long!) Be sure to reread some of the books, especially the picture books. As you read aloud the books, the children will become familiar with them and will be able to use them both for retelling and for independent reading over time.

Here is an annotated bibliography of children's books about names:

Picture Books Multicultural

Ashok by Any Other Name by Sandra S. Yamate. Polychrome Publishing Corporation, 1992.
    In this book, an Indian American boy wishes he had a name that sounded more "American." His classmates have trouble pronouncing his name and he feels self-conscious. This is a book many immigrant students will relate to.

The Day of Ahmed's Secret by Florence Parry Heide, et al. Houghton Mifflin, 1995.
    Ahmed, a young boy in Cairo, has a job of delivering bottles of propane gas throughout the busy streets. At the end of the book, he reveals his secret... he has learned to write his name. Young readers will delight in this story set in a land very different from their own.

Little Boy with Three Names: Stories of Taos Pueblo by Ann Nolan Clark. Kiva Publishing, 1999.
    This book for young children is written by a Newberry Award medallist and tells three stories about a child with three names- one Anglo, one Hispanic, and one Pueblo. He attends boarding school in the winter and returns home to his people in the summer. It is a book rich in Native American culture.

The Name Jar by Yangsook Choi. Knopf, 2001.
    Written by a Korean author, this book is about a student who just moved to the U.S. and is worried about the other students accepting her. Her name is hard to pronounce, so she tells them she will choose a name by the next week. Her classmates help her by putting new names in a jar. At the end of   the story, Unhei (Yoon-Hey) decides that the name she would like to be called is her Korean name.

Picture Books Fiction

A, My Name Is Alice by Jane Bayer. E.P. Dutton, 1992.
> This charming picture book illustrated by Steven Kellogg is an ABC book as well as a book about names. It's a version of the familiar jump rope game with a patterned text children love… A, my name is Alice and my husband's name is Alex. We come from Alaska and we sell apes.

A Porcupine Named Fluffy by Helen Lester. Houghton Mifflin, 1989.
> This porcupine has an unusual name that makes him feel different. But when he meets a misnamed rhinoceros, Hippo, he begins to accept his name.

Chrysanthemum by Kevin Henkes. Greenwillow, 1991.
> Chrysanthemum thinks her name is perfect until she begins kindergarten and is teased by her classmates for having such a long, unusual name. A caring teacher and loving parents support her and help her celebrate her unique name. In fact, the teacher begins a new trend by naming her new baby after a flower, too.

From Anne to Zach by Mary Jane Martin. Boyds Mills Press, 1996.
> This alphabet book uses children's names and rhymes to teach the letters.

Heart of a Tiger by Marsha Diane Arnold. Dial Books for Young Readers, 1995.
> This book tells the story of a small kitten, "Number Four," who searches for a name for his naming day. He follows a great Bengal tiger and saves his life to earn his new name, "Heart of a Tiger." It's a story of wisdom and courage.

How I Named the Baby by Linda Shute and Christy Grant. Albert Whitman & Co., 1993.
> James and his family are waiting for the new baby to arrive and try to think of a name. They talk about names for months. However, in the end the baby is born in June, which becomes the easiest name of all to choose. This book includes information from several countries on favorite names and their meanings.

Naming the Cat by Laurence Pringle. Walker & Co., 1997.
> A family adopts a black and white cat and must come up with a name for it. The new name is revealed at the end of the story after many several near disasters!

The Other Emily by Gibbs Davis, et al. Houghton Mifflin, 1990.
> Emily thinks she is the only one in the world with her name until she begins school. Many children and teachers will identify with the dilemma of duplicate first names in the classroom.

Santa's Book of Names by David McPhail. Little Brown & Co., 1993.
> Edward has trouble learning to read until Santa asks him to help. Santa has lost his glasses, and Edward must read the names listing all the gifts the children will receive. This holiday story will certainly delight young readers and highlights the importance of reading.

Easy Readers   Fiction

Hello, Biscuit by Alyssa Satin Capucilli. Harper Collins, 1998.
>   This book tells how Biscuit the dog got his name. Young readers will be delighted by this series of *I Can Read books.*

Nonfiction

103 Perfect Pet Names by Paul Meisel
>   This is a rhyming book that gives kids ideas for names for new pets. What a great book to have as a reference for story writing about animals or for naming that classroom pet!

A Name on the Quilt: A Story of Remembrance by Jeannine Atkins. Atheneum, 1999.
>   A family gathers to remember their Uncle Ron who died of AIDS. They make a quilt to commemorate his life and what he loved. The AIDS memorial quilt is mentioned at the end of the book.

A Pinky Is a Baby Mouse: And Other Baby Animal Names. Hyperion Press, 1999.
>   Here's another book of rhymes that introduces young readers to the interesting names of baby animals. It's set up in a guessing game format and includes many unusual vocabulary words.

The Wall by Eve Bunting. Clarion 1990.
>   A visit to the Vietnam Veterans Memorial acquaints a young boy with the grandfather he never knew. He and his dad search the wall to find the name of his granddad along with others looking for the names of loved ones.

Chapter Books   Grades 2-4

The Girl with 500 Middle Names by Margaret Peterson. Aladdin, 2001.
>   Janie's mom knits personalized sweaters in her spare time to sell to a specialty shop. However, when the family moves, the storeowner has found a cheaper source and returns the sweaters. Janie begins to wear the sweaters to her new school since her mom now can't afford to buy new school clothes. When the kids ask her about the sweaters, she tells them the names on the sweaters are her middle names. This is a story of friendship and family.

Just Like Mine by Gail Herman, et al. Yearling Books, 2001.
>   When Michael's mother remarries, his new last name will be Jordan and he's anything but Michael Jordan! Beginning chapter book readers will enjoy this amusing story.

No Copycats Allowed! by Bonnie B. Graves, et al. Hyperion, 1998.
>   Gabrielle is a third grader at a new school and has the challenge of both making new friends and the spelling of her long name. Children will enjoy the fast-paced story and will identify with the feelings of insecurity we've all faced at one time or another.

Teaching With Names in Shared Reading

Begin the year by doing *shared reading* with the large names charts in your classroom. Gather the children on the floor in your large group teaching area. Post a large names chart in this area. Point to each name on the chart with a small pointer and read the names and photos together. After reading, have volunteers come to the chart and find a specific name. Over time begin to use the category cards from *Sort the Names* (see pages 49-50). Help the children take turns finding a name that has four letters, a name that rhymes with *lamb* (*Sam*), a name that begins like *brown* (*Brian, Brendan*), a name that has *two claps* (two syllables), etc. As children become familiar with these tasks, place the Sort the Names bag into the *Names Work Station* (see page 22) for students to use for practice.

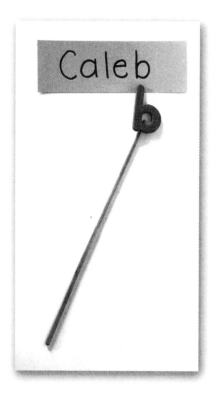

For kindergarten and first grade students, make special pointers from wooden chopsticks with a foam letter (such as, Lauri's *Avalanche of Letters*) glued to the end of each with epoxy glue or Tacky® glue. Have children take turns choosing a pointer, and then coming to the chart to point to a name that has that letter in it. Have the child name the letter, say the sound, and read the corresponding name.

For *shared reading* in grades K through 2, read poems with blanks into which children's names are inserted. See the following page for ideas on how to use these names poems. Have children take turns helping to point as you read the poems day after day. After reading, let students take turns finding high frequency words and familiar names.

When you teach with children's names, you will find that they learn many of the sounds of the letters. Be explicit in making connections between words you are reading in poems and big books and their own names. Point to and read the word in the *shared reading* text. Then point to and read the corresponding name on the names chart. For example as you read, *"to fetch a pail of water…,"* say *"water* (pointing to that word) *begins like William"* (pointing to his name on the large names chart by the big book easel). Remind children that they can use the names charts to help them with the first sound when they get stuck on a word. Make the small names charts (page 13) accessible to children during reading and writing to help them with new words.

Names Poems

Duplicate these poems in several ways.

Blackline masters of the poems can be found beginning on page 32.

1. Copy them onto chart paper with a thick black marker to use for shared reading. Laminate the chart paper so names can be added with a vis-à-vis pen.
2. Or copy them onto overhead transparencies. Put transparencies into clear plastic sleeves to protect them.
3. Or copy the poems, line by line, onto sentence strips. Write the children's names on individual sentence strips and use a pocket chart to fill the names in the blanks.

Always read the poems together many times in shared reading before having students read these on their own! You might add these poems to the child's poetry folder (a spiral notebook with poems glued in and illustrated by the student).

2nd grade note:

Have students write poems about their own names.

Include first and last names. Have them copy the poems onto sentence strips for others to read. This is purposeful handwriting practice. Here are some ideas for writing names poems. Model with your own name first!

1. Write an acrostic poem. Make each letter stand for something you like to do.
   - D designing things
   - E eating watermelon
   - B buying accessories

2. Write a poem with clues. Don't give your name. Let others guess. Rhyme, if you'd like.
   - I have blue eyes and short brown hair.
   - You'll find me reading anywhere.
   - I like to make fun things for you.
   - I can always find something to do.
   - Who am I?

Teaching with Names in Guided Reading

After familiarizing children with the names chart in shared reading, use it as a tool for teaching in guided reading. Have a small names chart on your guided reading table where you will meet with the students in a small group. You might attach a back to the chart and create a stand-up tent, as shown, or put it in a desktop stand and desktop center chart.

Also have highlighter tape available. You might highlight a beginning or ending letter or a chunk (a group of letters that makes a specific sound) to remind students of what they already know in the names.

In guided reading you will work with one small group at a time reading the same book. As children read, remind them to use the names chart to help themselves if they get stuck. Tell them they can use a name to help them remember the sound a letter (or a chunk) makes. You might demonstrate this before children begin reading by saying something like, "I'm stuck on this word… I can look at the names chart and find a name that starts with the same letter as this word… it begins like *William*. It must say 'w…' Now I remember… It's *with*." You might use highlighter tape to make the *W* in *William* stand out and remind the children to use the beginning sounds they already know in their names.

Mrs. Terry's Class

Briana	Alvin
Chrisshunda	Dior
Delila	Erick
Kourtney	Jordan
Jasmine	Justin
Jessica	Max
Monica	Mohammed
Rebecca	Noman
Shyanne	Terran
Tara	Terreous
Vivian	William
Zoya	

As children read their books, listen in to their reading and prompt as needed. Remember that you are acting as a "coach," helping and guiding them, not giving them every word they get stuck on! Encourage them to use the names chart. Some prompts you might use are listed below:

- If you can read *Briana*, you can read *brown*.
- That word has *on* in it, just like in *Monica*.
- You can figure that word out. It starts like (*Shyanne*).
- You can find that *or* chunk in a name on our names chart. Yes, *or* like in *Jordan* and *Dior*. Now you try the word.
- Find a name that starts like that word. Now try it.
- Use the names chart to help yourself.
- What did you try? How did the names chart help you?

Teaching with Names in Independent Reading

In independent reading, children should be reading books they can read with little or no help. They should practice reading familiar books or books that are easy for them so they can develop fluency and phrasing. It is helpful to have each child keep an individual book bag or book box. One way to do this that involves little cost or space is to give each child a large ziploc bag as a place to keep books for independent reading. Write each child's name on a blank index card with a thick black marker and have the child decorate it with crayons. Staple it to the top inside the bag. Inside the book bag, place books already read in guided reading, an ABC chart, a reading log (if students are keeping these), and a small names chart. This names chart can simply be an 8½" x 11" paper copy stored in a clear plastic sleeve for protection; or it can be a laminated sheet.

Before children read in independent reading, remind them that they can use the names chart to help them with a tricky word. Tell them that's why the names chart is in their book bag! They will use the names charts only if the teacher has modeled how to do this.

As you walk around the classroom while children read independently, you may have to prompt them occasionally to use the names chart if they get stuck on a word. Praise any students you see doing this on their own. This will encourage both that child and others to do the same thing to help themselves. You might use the same prompts found in guided reading, on the previous page.

In the classroom library, you might put a large chart with children's names written on the left hand side. Provide blank sticky notes and show students how to jot down the titles of favorite books on sticky notes and post these by their names for others to see. This is a great way to recommend books to others using the children's names and may aid in student book selection.

2nd grade note:

Have children write recommendations to each other. Be sure they sign their names. They can write these on a message board in the classroom library.

Teaching with Names in the Basal

Any activity you use for teaching with names in this book can be applied to teaching with a basal reading series.

During shared reading, you can look for poems in the basal that use names and copy them onto chart paper. Supplement the poems and stories in the basal by using some of the names poems in this book. Remember that a basal has more than you could possibly use in one year and that it's okay to use other pieces along with it to best meet the needs of all the students in your classroom.

Look for stories in the basal about names that can be used during read aloud or small group reading. Especially in the first book in a basal series, there are often stories about back to school and getting to know each other. The teacher's edition may yield additional resources for work with names.

The same ideas presented in the sections in this book for guided reading and for writing can be applied if you use a basal. Simply adapt them to the particular stories and texts you are reading and writing with your boys and girls. Use the same direct teaching demonstrations and explicit language as recommended in this book.

If you teach with a basal, you should still have a large names chart in your classroom for large group instruction and small names charts for small group instruction and independent work.

If you have children in your classroom from other countries, you will find the ideas on *Teaching with Names from Other Languages* to be helpful.

You will find that using names improves children's understanding of language and how it works, no matter what materials you are using for your instruction. The child's name is the first word most children learn to read and write and is the most powerful piece of print for them to use.

Teaching with Names by Writing

Use children's names to teach correct letter formation. Young children should be instructed to write their names with strokes going from top to bottom and left to right. Many children are simply *drawing* their names rather than writing them. Teachers *should* teach children the correct way to form letters for writing fluency.

As you sit beside the child, print the child's name in thick black letters on a large sheet of paper or a large index card. (If the child has poor motor control, use a larger piece of paper.) As you write, tell the child how you are forming the letters. "Make a capitol *B*. Pull the line down. Then lift your pencil and start at the top again. Make one bump to the middle. Then make another bump under it. Now the *i*. Pull the line down. Put a dot on top. Now the *l*. Pull the line down. Make the last *l*. Pull the line down." Then give the child an assortment of colored crayons. Let the child trace the name over and over again using a different color each time he finishes the word. Have the child repeat your directions for writing each letter to help the child remember **how** to form each one. These are sometimes called "rainbow names."

Once children are fluent in writing their names, use names to make class books and individual books. Use the blacklines on pages 42-44. Put these books in the classroom library for independent reading.

Use the names chart to model for students how to "stretch out" words and write the sounds they hear. Show them what they already know in the names and how to apply that to their writing. For example, "I want to write *toy*. I can stretch out that word and hear the sounds… *t*… like in *Tamara*. I'll write a *t* first. *T-oy*. *Oy* is in *Zoya's* name. I'll write *oy* next. That's *toy!*" After seeing many models, children will learn to use their names to help themselves spell other words.

Have a small names chart posted in your writing center to help children with spelling each other's names and in writing down sounds they hear. Also place a small names chart in each child's writing folder to use during independent writing.

2nd grade note:

Some children will still need instruction with letter formation. Using their names is a good starting point. 2nd graders love to make books, too!

Daily Sign-In

In place of an attendance check, have children sign in daily when they enter the classroom to show that they are present. In kindergarten, sign-in gives students an opportunity to practice writing their names and learn correct letter formation. In first grade, it gives children the opportunity to write their names and collect data for graphs or ongoing projects. Middle and last names can be added as children develop. In second grade, sign-in might be used to transition to cursive writing later in the year. Your signature is the one item you must write in cursive in real life!

First, prepare sheets of 8½" x 11" piece of paper at several tables. At the top of the paper, type, *Please sign in.* At the bottom of the page type, *Thank you.* Draw a line for each signature. (Sample blackline master for sign-in can be found on page 45). Assign a table to each group of 5-6 students. At each table, include a sentence strip with each child's name on it for a model of correct letter formation. As children become more adept at sign-in, a question of the day can be added. You can provide *yes/no* boxes or leave space for more extended answers. This procedure can be linked to what you are studying in math, science, and/or social studies.

Kindergarten Sign-In Example

1st Grade Sign-In Example

The following resources will be helpful in learning more about sign-in:
Joyful Learning in Kindergarten by Bobbi Fisher, Heineman, 1998.
Literacy's Beginnings by McGee and Richgels, Allyn and Bacon, 1996.

Sample Questions for Sign-In

QUESTIONS with YES/NO Answers:

Do you like pizza?
Do you like milk?
Do you like to watch TV?
Do you like school?
Do you have a dog?
Do you have a cat?
Do you have a brother?
Do you have a sister?
Can you ride a bike?
Can you whistle?

Can you count to 10?
Can you tie your shoes?
Can you skip?
Can you snap your fingers?
Did you ride the bus today?
Did you walk to school today?
Did you wear a coat today?
Did you wear a white shirt today?
Did you eat breakfast today?
Are you 5 years old?

QUESTIONS with Single-Word Answers:

How old are you?
How many brothers do you have?
How many sisters do you have?
What color are your eyes?
What color is your hair?
What color are your shoes?
What is your favorite food?
What is your favorite number?
What is your favorite sport?
What is your favorite animal?

Who is your favorite relative?
Who do you like to play with?
What time do you go to bed?
What time do you get up?
What do you like for breakfast?
What do you like for dessert?
What is your favorite kind of ice cream?
What is your favorite candy?
What do you like to do at recess?
What is your favorite toy?

QUESTIONS with Extended Answers:

What street do you live on?
What place would you like to visit?
What is your favorite movie?
What is your favorite TV show?
What is your favorite book?
What do you like to do after school?
What do you think a _____ is?
What do you think _____ means?
Where were you born?
What would you like to learn about?

Who would you like to meet?
Who is your favorite author?
What would you like to do when you grow up?
What did you learn yesterday?
What did you do this weekend?
What will you do this weekend?
Why did you come to school today?
What do you know about _____?
When is your birthday?
What would you like for your birthday?

Teaching with Names in Word Study

Use the children's names to model word sorts. Make names cards as described on page 3. You may want to include the children's photos on their sorting cards to help them learn each other's names. Use black ink for all names so children can use the names flexibly for sorting. If you choose to make boys' names one color and girls' another at the beginning of the year as a scaffold for helping young students find their names, you may want to make another set of names cards using black ink later in the year.

Show children how to sort boys' and girls' names first. Sit in a large circle and read each name card together. Then together sort them into two columns, one with names of boys and the other of girls. After sorting, always point and read the names together. Make extra copies of the names cards and let small groups work together just to get the idea of sorting. Have them do the exact sort you modeled. Over time, introduce different kinds of sorts using their names. Use the *Sort the Names* ideas on page 26. Then let students do the sorting activities independently at the word study center.

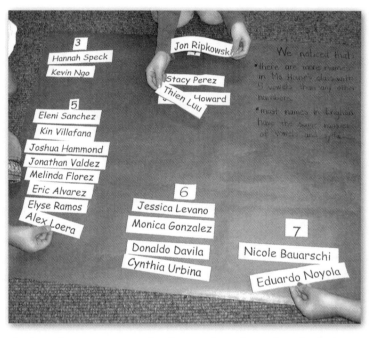

2nd graders sort names by the number of vowels... in their first names, in their last names, in their whole names.

Use the names on the word wall and names in poems during shared reading to do word study as well. Have children use highlighter tape to highlight phonetic elements being studied.

2nd grade note:

Use first and second names in the names sorts. Have children write about what they learned by sorting the names.

Teaching with Names from Other Languages

If you have children in your classroom from other countries, use their names to teach how language differs from country to country. You might do a sort of names with English sounds, names with Spanish sounds, and names with Vietnamese sounds (depending on the children's names in your class). Help the children to be proud of their names; celebrate our diversity using their names!

As you place names on the word wall, you might be concerned about placing *Julio* under the *Jj* card since it makes a different sound than the English one. If so, you might type the *J* in Julio's name in a different color as a signal that it makes a different sound than the English one. This may also help Julio with the difference between the Spanish and English sounds if he is transitioning to English. Other letters to highlight for Spanish speakers are the *i* (which makes the long *e* sound) and *e* (which makes the long *a* sound) to help them with the English sounds. Ask your second language learners to help you highlight the sounds that are different from English to help them. Some English names have unusual sounds that you might want to highlight also, such as the *i* in *Tina*.

Help children be proud of their native languages. Show them how many of our English words come from other lands as well. For example, *pizza* and *piano* are from Italian, and *rodeo* is from the Spanish language. Ask children to teach the class how to say their names with their native sounds. Work hard to pronounce their names correctly. Don't try to "Americanize" their names. Use some of the multicultural picture books noted on page 8 during read aloud to help children from other lands feel good about their names.

Spanish Names

Julio
Maria

English Names

Jessica
Billy

Vietnamese Names

Thien

2nd grade note:

For homework, have children find out how they got their names. Then have them write about this and share with the class.

Making Names Books with Children

On pages 42-44 are blackline masters to help you make names books with your children. You'll notice that the text begins at the top of the page. This is designed to help your students learn to move from the top to the bottom of the page. The child should write his/her name in the first blank and the name of a classmate in the second blank. There is additional space for early/transitional writers to add another sentence or two about their friend, if they'd like. Children should also be encouraged to add a drawing of themselves and their friends. You might also consider adding a photo of the child and their classmate to the bottom of the page as an illustration. Each student can make a page for the book and you can bind these into a class book for everyone to read and enjoy. Be sure to add an attractive student-made cover with a title, such as "Mrs. Diller's Class Names Book."

You can also place blank sheets in your writing center for children to use to make their own individual books. They could use 3 or 4 of the pages to create their own names books. Be sure to place a names photo chart in the writing center to help them.

Here are some samples of what the pages might look like when finished:

class names book

individual names book

Names Work Stations

The Names Work Stations can be set up in the ABC center or they can be their own separate stations. Place each in a Ziploc freezer bag. Make a label for each bag with a 4½″ x 12″ piece of colored construction paper. Use a different colored label for each bag. Glue the direction card (ie, *Sort the Names*) and the matching photo to the label; then laminate and staple to the top of the Ziploc bag. Use the blackline masters on pages 46-48 or substitute your own digital photos of children from your classroom doing each activity. Place the materials needed inside the bag. Begin with just one activity or type of material in each bag. Introduce one new item at a time to add novelty and keep this station interesting over time.

Make a names/photo chart and place inside each *Names Work Station* bag. See page 49 for a template. Place the names in ABC order. You might place the boys' names on one side and girls' on the other. Mount the chart on colored construction paper to match the label and help keep supplies organized. Place names to the left and glue photos to the right. Take pictures with a digital camera or use school pictures.

Show the children how to use the *Names Work Stations* by playing the games with them in large group first, and then in a small group. Then place them in the center for independent practice.

Names/Photo Chart

name	photo	name	photo
name	photo	name	photo
name	photo	name	photo
name	photo	name	photo
name	photo	name	photo
name	photo	name	photo

Beyond the Names Chart 22

NOTE: Use first and last names in mid-1st grade and early 2nd grade.

Sample Modeled Lesson for Names Work Station

1. Set a purpose: *We're going to learn to write each other's names so we can write notes to each other.*
2. Explore the bag of materials together.
3. Read the directions and pictures together.
4. Model the use of materials explicitly.
5. Demonstrate what to do in case of problems.
6. Model clean up.
7. Have two students demonstrate and get feedback from the rest of the class.
8. Two at a time, let children practice with the names work station materials in this bag.
9. Add one new thing at a time, over time.

Things to Model in a Mini-Lesson

What problems might arise?	Mini lesson solution
Kids mix up the pieces in the different bags.	Model how to put materials away.
Kids yell out asking how to spell each other's names.	Model how to find the answer. Place a names/photo chart in each bag.
Kids have trouble with rings that name cards are attached to.	Model how to put cards on the ring. Be sure to use easy-to-open rings.
Kids don't put lids back on the markers tightly.	Model how to listen for the "click" when putting on the lids.
Kids interrupt the teacher and ask for her help.	Model appropriate ways to get help.
Kids don't put materials back in the right bag.	Model how to put materials away. Code materials with colored dots.

Match the Names

Materials needed:

- Photo of each child
- Child's name printed in black ink on sentence strip
- Sentence about child, including name and picture
- Names/photo chart (for checking)

To prepare:

- Take a digital or Polaroid photo of each child, or use school pictures.
- Print or type a matching name card for each child.
- Each child dictates a sentence about himself/herself which the teacher prints or types onto a long card or sentence strip.

To play:

- The child matches a photo to the person's picture.
- The child matches a photo to the sentence about that person.
- Check answers with the name chart in the bag.

2nd grade note:

Have students write their own sentences about themselves to use at this station.

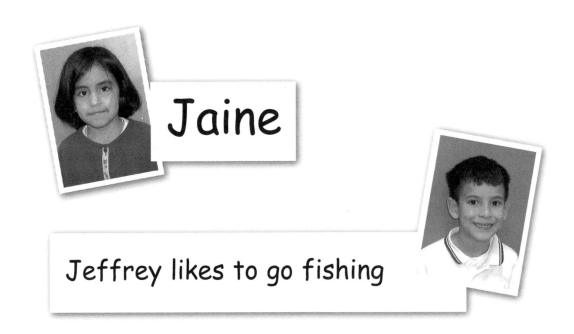

Make the Names

Materials needed:
- Name puzzles in white envelopes
- Individual name cards on a 1" book ring
- Wikki Stix and plain placemat
- Magnetic letters and cookie sheet
- Sponge ABCs, paint, and paper
- Letter stamps, washable ink pads, and paper
- Link and spell letters and magnetic surface
- Letter tiles
- Alpha-Snaps
- Names/photo chart (for checking)

To prepare:
- To make a name puzzle, type each child's name *twice* in the font Comic Sans bold, size 72, and type a space between each letter. Then cut the names out. Glue one to the back of a business size white envelope. Laminate it and cut it open at the back slit. Laminate the other copy of the name and cut it apart letter by letter. Store the individual letters in the envelope.
- To make name cards, print or type each name on a 3" x 5" card and punch a hole in the upper left-hand corner. Place on a 1" book ring.

To play:
- The child makes a name by matching the letters on the envelope in the name puzzle.
- The child makes a name by spelling it with assorted materials. Change the materials periodically to keep this activity fresh and novel. Display the names creations!

Sort the Names

Materials needed:
- Names typed onto cards, one name per card (might include photo)
- Sorting cards

To prepare:
- Type or print each name onto a card. Include photo if you'd like.
- Prepare sorting category cards using the cards on pages 50-51. For example, have the children sort names by boys and girls using the category cards with those labels on page 50. Or have them sort by number of letters in each name using the number labels on that same page. They might also sort by number of syllables (using the numbered clapping cards on page 51) or by the beginning sound (using *Begin with ___* or *End with ___*).

To play:
- Do one sort at a time. Begin with sorting boys' and girls' names, the easiest sort, just to teach the sorting process. Show children how to:
    1. Deal the cards to group members.
    2. Place the category cards.
    2. Sort the names cards under the category cards.
    3. Read the names cards one at a time down the column.
- Introduce other sorts over time.
- Let children invent their own sorts.
- In mid-1st grade and early 2nd grade you might have them record their sorts by copying the words onto paper in columns. Then have them write about the kind of sort they did and what they noticed. (For example, I sorted boys' and girls' names. I noticed that there were twice as many boys' names.)
- *Be sure children read the names each time they sort!*

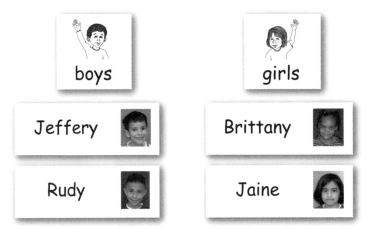

2nd grade note:
Use first and last names in the sorts. Let students come up with their own ways of sorting. Have them tell the class how they sorted and what they learned.

Read the Names

Names Poem:

Materials needed:
- names poems
- individual names on cards (to fit in blank spaces on names poems)
- magnetic letters for *Patty-Cake* and *There Was a Teacher* poems
- class names/photo chart (for reference to check names)

To prepare:
- Copy each poem on pages 33-41 onto white paper. Glue each poem to tagboard and laminate. Make individual name cards to fit in the blanks in the poems. Include magnetic letters for *Patty-Cake* (capital letters that begin each child's name) and *There Was a Teacher* poems (letters that spell the teacher's name).

To play:
- Children put an individual name card in each blank and read the poem. They can interchange the names and read the poems over and over again. When reading *Patty-Cake*, children put a magnetic letter in the blank that starts the name they are using in the poem. When they read *There Was a Teacher*, they use magnetic letters to spell the teacher's name in the blanks.

Picture Books/Student-made Books:

Materials needed:
- trade books with children's names in them
- student-made names books
- precut highlighter tape on an index card
- blank paper and pencils
- class names/photo chart (for reference to check names)

To prepare:
- Find picture books and/or student-made books that include the names of students in your classroom. For example, use *Alexander and the Terrible, Horrible, No Good, Very Bad Day* by Judith Viorst, if you have a child named *Alexander* in your class. Student-made books work well if you have trouble finding trade books that use your students' names. Precut highlighter tape and place it on a blank index card.

To play:
- Have students read the book or tell the story (depending on their reading levels). Then have them find the child's name and use highlighter tape to mark it. On a piece of paper, they might write the book title and list all the different names they found in it, including the one belonging to the child in your classroom. When finished, have them remove the highlighter tape and place it back on the index card.

Names Books with Names Puzzles:

Materials needed:
- teacher-made names books
- names puzzles (the letters that spell the name of the child written letter-by-letter on cardstock and a card with the child's whole name on it)
- 1" book rings
- library pockets for storage container
- class names/photo chart (for reference to check names)

To prepare:
- To prepare: create teacher-made names books. Make several pages with 6" x 9" colored construction paper. On each page glue a photo of a child and a sentence telling about the child, as shown. Use text that matches the level of your students. For example, in kindergarten write *I see Monica.* In grade 1, use *Monica is my new friend.* In grade 2, the sentence might be written by the child: *My name is Monica and I am a really good swimmer.*
- On the right hand side of each page of these books for K–1, attach a library pocket. Make a name puzzle to put in each pocket: write the child's name on a large card and each letter of the name on a smaller card. Attach all these cards with a 1" book ring to make a name puzzle and store it in the pocket, as shown below.

To play:
- First, children read each page. Then they take the matching name from the pocket and match it to the name on that page. Finally, they take the names puzzle from the pocket, open the book ring to release the letters and name, and line up the letters to make the name. When finished, they put the letters and name back on the ring and return it to the pocket.

Write the Names

Materials needed:

- Salt tray
- File folder post office (see below)
- Magna Doodle
- Black paper and colored chalk
- Little chalkboard and tube moistener from an office supply store
  (Tell the children it's a "water pen.")
- Dry erase board and dry erase markers

To prepare:

- Place one of the materials or materials sets above into the ziploc bag. Include a names/photo chart.
- To make a salt tray, put a thin layer of salt in a plastic deli container lid. On 5" x 8" index cards print each child's name in large black letters. Place a card under the lid and have the child trace the name. The black letters will lightly show through the salt making it easy for the child to trace.
- Fill a tube moistener (used for moistening envelopes and stamps) partway with water. Have the child write the names on a small chalkboard with the "water pen." Or they can write on a big chalkboard. The water will show up on the dark surface of the chalkboard and evaporate quickly.
- Put several different colors of chalk in a small plastic bag. Put that bag and some strips of black construction paper into the larger ziploc bag.
- To make a file folder post office, use a file folders with library pockets attached. Write a child's name on a library pocket to form the "mailbox." You'll probably need to make two of these so each child in your class has a mailbox. Have the children write notes to their friends using the names. Then they place the notes in the mailbox of the appropriate child.

To play:

- The child uses the materials in the Write the Names bag.

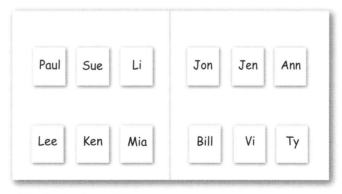

File Folder Post Office

Guess the Names

Materials needed:
- Masking devices
- Name riddles
- Names cards
- Names/photo chart (for checking)

To prepare:
- Write each child's name on sentence strip in black ink to make a name card.
- Then make a masking device. Use a 6" x 10" piece of black construction paper. Fold it in half lengthwise; then fold it in half again lengthwise. Cut out a window, as shown.
- Then unfold and tape along the bottom edge with Scotch tape. Place a name card inside it. Then cut another piece of black construction paper 3" x 10". Insert it into the windowed piece as a sliding device. It should move back and forth to cover and uncover parts of the name. Make a separate masking device for each name.
- To make names riddles for readers, write a riddle on a card about each child. Include clues to help the reader guess that child's identity. Put the child's name on the back to make it self-correcting.

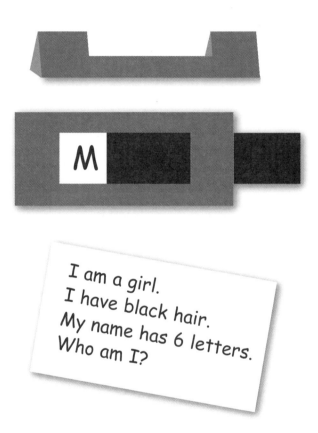

To play:
- The child takes a masking device with the name in it and tries to guess the name as he uncovers one letter at a time. Provide a names/photo chart for self checking.
- Readers can read and guess the riddles. They can also write their own riddles about themselves and/or other students in the classroom.

Teaching with Names in Math

Counting and sorting activities can be done with names. You can count the number of boys' and girls' names on the names chart. The numbers may change throughout the year as children move in and out of your classroom. You can write number statements about the numbers in your class.

Do sorts based upon the number of letters in each child's name. Label each sort with the numeral that represents the number of letters.

Have children look for patterns in their names. Ask them to look for patterns with tall and short letters, vowels and consonants, etc.

Jake tall, short, tall, short
Pam consonant, vowel, consonant

> Today we have more boys than girls.
> There are 8 boys and 11 girls.

2	3	4	5
Vi	Tom	Alex	Debra
	Lin	Will	Sally

Use children's names in daily word problems. Each day write a new story. Use the same pattern for a while to help beginning readers. Have the child help tell the story as you write. For example, Kenneth has one sister and two brothers. How many brothers and sisters does he have in all?

Older children can also find the value of their names by assigning a number to each letter from 1-26. Have them add to find out how much their name is worth. Let them use counters if they need them. Create a chart with the students first to use for reference:

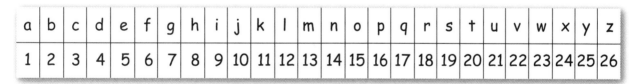

a	b	c	d	e	f	g	h	i	j	k	l	m	n	o	p	q	r	s	t	u	v	w	x	y	z
1	2	3	4	5	6	7	8	9	10	11	12	13	14	15	16	17	18	19	20	21	22	23	24	25	26

$$Jake = 10 + 1 + 11 + 5 = 27$$

Create charts and graphs using children's names. Find out: favorite foods, colors, pets, authors, TV shows, movies, number of brothers, sisters, pets, etc

2nd grade note:

Have children write word problems for each other using their names.

Blacklines

Names Poems

NOTE: Put the child's name in each blank and sing it over and over again. Or put magnetic letters in each space and spell the child's name.

Patty - Cake

Patty - cake, patty – cake

Baker's man .

Bake me a cake as fast as you can .

Pat it and prick it

And mark it with a ___

And put it in the oven

For _____ and me !

Happy Birthday to You

Happy birthday to you.

Happy birthday to you.

Happy birthday , dear _____

Happy birthday to you.

Jack and Jill

_____ and _____ went up the hill.

To fetch a pail of water.

_____ fell down.

And broke his crown.

And _____ came tumbling after.

There Was a Teacher

There was a teacher had a kid

And _____ was his name-o.

_____   _____

_____   _____

_____   _____

And _____ was his name-o.

Jack Be Nimble

_____ be nimble.

_____ be quick.

_____ jump

Over the candlestick.

May I Have a Turn?

———————————— , ————————————

May I have a turn?

Yes, you may.

That's how we learn.

Just Like Me

_____ can hop everywhere.

_____ can sit on a chair.

_____ can clap, 1 2 3.

_____ can read

Just like me!

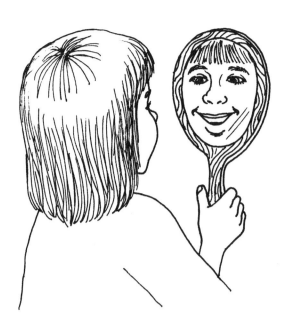

Look in the Mirror

_____ looked in the mirror

And what did she see?

_____ saw a big smile

And said, "I like me!"

In the Box

_____ in the box.

_____ in the box.

Wake up. Wake up.

Somebody knocks.

One time. Two times.

Three times. Four.

_____ pops out of the

Little round door.

1. Cut out the shaded parts.
2. Throw them away.
3. In the middle box, write your name.
4. Fold in on the dotted lines.
5. On each part write a clue about yourself.
6. Have others read your clues and try to guess who you are.

My name is

_____

I am _____
I like _____.

My name is _____ and I like _____.

Please sign in.

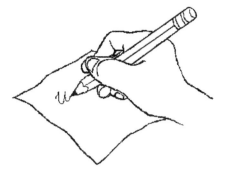

_____

_____

_____

_____

_____

Thank you.

Match the names.

Make the names.

Sort the names.

Read the names.

Write the names.

Guess the names.

Names/Photo Chart

boys

girls

Number of Syllables

1	2
3	4
5	6
7	8
9	10

Number of Syllables

# 1 clap 	# 2 claps 
# 3 claps 	# 4 claps 
# 5 claps 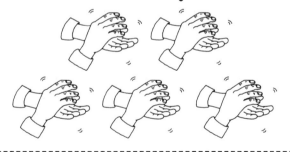	# 6 claps 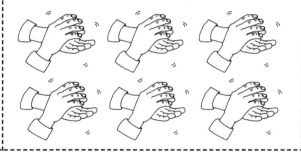

Beginning/Ending Sounds

# Begin with _____	# End with _____

Teaching Resource Center

P.O. Box 82777, San Diego, CA 92138

The following materials have been referred to in this book. To order or find more information out about these and other products:

Call 1-800-833-3389
or visit our website: www.trcabc.com

Avalanche of Letters
Big Book Easel
Blank Flash Cards
Book Pouches
Desktop Pocket Chart
Desktop Stand
Dry-erase Markers
Fabric Word Wall
Highlighter Tape
I Can Read Books
Kid-sized Erasers
Magna Doodle
Magnetic Letters
Markboards
Pocket Charts
Sentence Strips